Understanding SECURIT
TRUST choice
B·A·L·A·N·C·E Joy
Happiness Accord Blessing
TRANQUILLITY
Freedom
MATURITY LOVE SURPRISE!
Zest harmony
cheer
peace C·A·L·M life Enthusiasm
HONOUR
BLISS Delight QUIET
comfort pleasure
FRESHNESS TENDERNESS
Laughter GROWTH fruition
HEALTH sunshine

Text copyright © 1994 Jean Watson
Illustrations copyright © 1994 Jane Hughes
This edition copyright © 1994 Lion Publishing

The author asserts the moral right
to be identified as the author of this work

Published by
**Lion Publishing plc**
Sandy Lane West, Oxford, England
ISBN 0 7459 2836 6
**Albatross Books Pty Ltd**
PO Box 320, Sutherland, NSW 2232, Australia
ISBN 0 7324 0862 8

First edition 1994

A catalogue record for this book is available
from the British Library

Library of Congress CIP Data applied for

Printed and bound in Singapore

# The Spirit of

# LOVE

*to say you care*

JEAN
WATSON

Illustrated by Jane Hughes

A LION BOOK

# INTRODUCTION

*One day our small son told me, 'I love you two hundred much!' We were on a great shoe-buying adventure and the little boy was full of joy and excitement as we sat in the shoe-shop waiting to be served. On hearing my son's remark, the woman sitting opposite caught my eye and, with a sideways glance at the morose adolescent beside her, commented wryly, 'Treasure that!' I did. I do.*

*Words can mean so much. Words of love and compassion, welcome and invitation, understanding and affirmation. How sad when words which people longed to hear during their lifetime are only said at their funeral services!*

*But words need the back-up of attitude, atmosphere and action. In some homes endearments ring very hollow because of the tone and context in which they are uttered, while in others a friendly punch, or just eye contact, can convey a wealth of affection.*

*Thoughtful actions, touch, body language, and what we give of ourselves can speak volumes. In this high-tech age we need good relationships more than ever. Happily, we can make technology work for − rather than against − these by adding loving, creative, human touches to our cards, gifts, letters, phone calls, faxes. They can make all the difference between merely existing, and celebrating life.*

*In this book I explore different aspects of love's medium and message, its content and effect, and also its cost. I am not in any doubt about this, having experienced my own suffering and shared that of others at times.*

*But it's those who have paid the price who have the most to give. And God, who is love, needs to play a crucial part in all this — if love is to be the many-splendoured thing it was meant to be.*

*As the poet Auden said, 'We must love one another or die' — if not physically, then spiritually and psychologically.*

*So, in the words of the old Puritan greeting: 'More love, sister! More love, brother!'*

*Yes?*

*Yes!*

**Jean Watson**

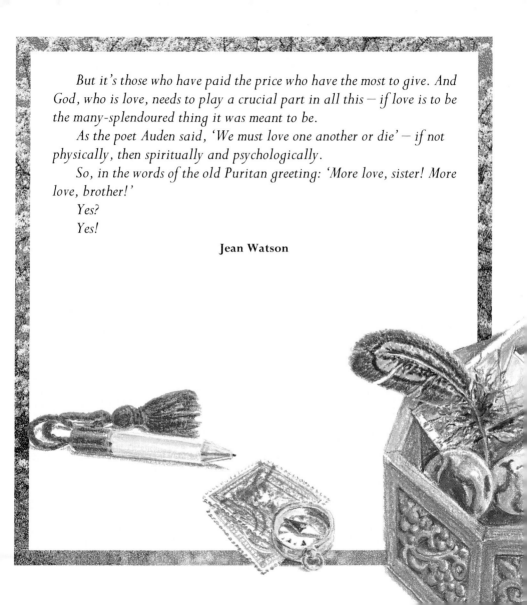

# FREE TO BE ME

I was rather slow in coming to a sense of my own identity. One reason was that I was sent to boarding school at an early age. When you are in an institution, you can miss out on many things which happen naturally in a good home. For example, you are rarely asked what you want or think or how you feel, because the focus necessarily is on the community rather than the individual. And the way children tend to respond to this situation is either to conform, and remain emotionally underdeveloped, or to buck the system and become over-assertive.

For me, as for others, this situation was, in time, remedied by the love of family and friends. Their attention and affection helped me to feel 'real' – a valuable person in my own right. And this human love gave reality to what I had always been taught about God loving and valuing me.

As we become more aware of what is or isn't 'us', our views and behaviour begin to reflect this greater consistency, instead of being 'all over the place'. And when we no longer feel the need to be anyone else's clone, we are able to form better relationships. Other people's opinions are no longer such a threat: we are freer to agree or disagree, and more able to cope when something challenging or hurtful is said.

Growing into wholeness through love is, of course, an ongoing process. And progress will depend on the kind of love experienced. Receiving God's love, reflected in the world and in people we are close to and trust, is the best way to ensure steady and continuous growth in our identity and relationships.

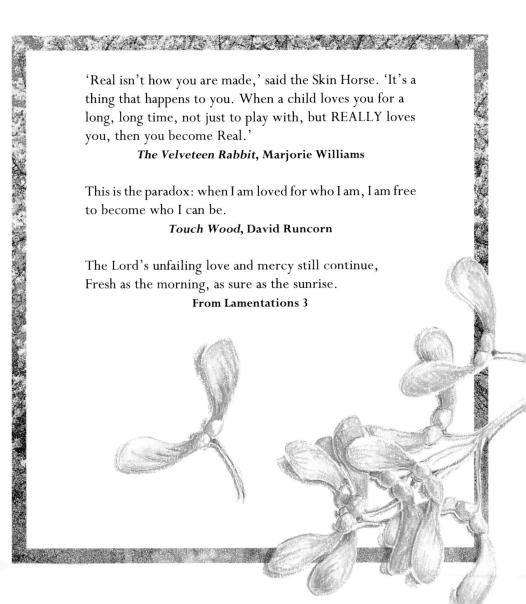

'Real isn't how you are made,' said the Skin Horse. 'It's a thing that happens to you. When a child loves you for a long, long time, not just to play with, but REALLY loves you, then you become Real.'

**The Velveteen Rabbit, Marjorie Williams**

This is the paradox: when I am loved for who I am, I am free to become who I can be.

**Touch Wood, David Runcorn**

The Lord's unfailing love and mercy still continue,
Fresh as the morning, as sure as the sunrise.

**From Lamentations 3**

# TRUE VALUE

Many teachers will say how important it is that children feel valued, not because of what they do or happen to be good at, but simply for *themselves*.

Those who feel of little value seem to respond in one of several ways, according to temperament. There are the more assertive, outgoing ones who – metaphorically if not literally – toss their heads and produce defiant 'see if I care' behaviour; there are the eager-to-please brigade, who engage in merit-building in an attempt to earn their worth; and there are the more introverted, timid children who accept their lack of value without resistance, and respond by virtually disappearing into the background.

Children do not automatically grow out of these attitudes and kinds of behaviour, as we know by looking around and within! We all need to experience the love of family, friends and 'significant others', who convey that we are of value by showing us affection, listening attentively to us, assuring us that they understand, and finding ways to encourage us.

This can disperse our anger, and lift us out of hopelessness and apathy. Then our time and energy can be for ourselves and for others, since now that we value ourselves, we value them too. And in valuing others, and reflecting God's love, we can ensure that compassion and justice prevail in all our relationships.

Look at the birds: they do not sow seeds, gather a harvest and put it in barns; yet your Father in heaven takes care of them! Aren't you worth much more than birds?

**From Matthew 6**

The value of any human being does not come from his goodness, or his creativity, his contribution to the state, the economy, the size of his bank account or even the number of his press clippings. His value is because he carries in his whole being the image of God.

***Beyond Identity*, Dick Keyes**

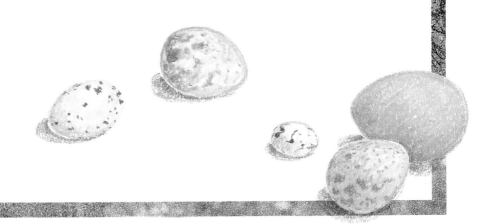

# INTEGRITY

Love is popularly misconceived as a mysterious, all-consuming force which sweeps aside every other consideration; one before which mere human beings are powerless.

But real love is an expression of the whole, integrated person – will, conscience, mind and spirit as well as feelings. True love is reflected in action, not just emotion. Then it can be good and tough enough to stand for right against wrong: refusing to take easy but second-rate options or to achieve its ends through force; wanting the best for others, while respecting their rights and freedoms.

Those who are parents need loving integrity. To say 'no' to our children, when it is right. Or to stand back and let them take the consequences of their own choices and actions. This may well disqualify us from entering any 'popular parent' contests, but so be it! The learning and growth of our children through these experiences must matter more than that.

It takes integrity, too, when we are looking after adults. We need to respect, and not to manipulate them; to stay with them and not to give up when situations get hard.

Clearly, loving integrity is not easy to offer. Nor, indeed, easy to receive. But with God we can develop this strong, true, unselfish love – reflecting, however imperfectly, something of his way of loving us all.

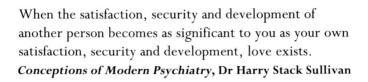

When the satisfaction, security and development of
another person becomes as significant to you as your own
satisfaction, security and development, love exists.
*Conceptions of Modern Psychiatry*, **Dr Harry Stack Sullivan**

If you love someone, you will never do him wrong.
**From Romans 13**

Genuine love is an expression of productiveness and
implies care, respect, responsibility and knowledge. It
is . . . an active striving for the growth and happiness of the
loved person, rooted in one's capacity to love.
*The Art of Loving*, **Erich Fromm**

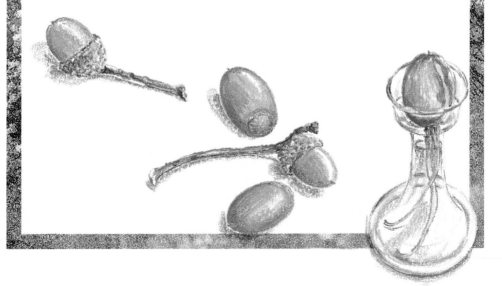

# LOVE HURTS

Anguish is always possible where there is love, and the greater the love, the deeper the anguish. It comes when loved ones suffer or are separated from us. When people are in difficulties or make a mess of things, when they fail to reach their true potential. And if they stop loving us, or if they hurt and reject us, it tears us apart.

Anguish may come through those we have personally looked after – a child, a pupil, an apprentice, an older relative. If they use their freedom unwisely and make destructive choices, it is bad enough. Seeing them suffer as a result is even worse – particularly if we cannot do anything for them, because they have moved away from us physically or, worse still, have cut themselves off from us emotionally.

The anguish for us is the fact of their pain, compounded, in some cases, by our frustrated love which couldn't protect them and can't care for them in the way we long to do. Time was, perhaps, when we were able to help them avoid mistakes, or when a kiss would have made everything all right again. Not any more!

In one such moment of anguish, it came to me, almost like a revelation, that God must be a parent in pain! And I suddenly felt very close to him. I also felt, presumptuous as this may sound, a sense of protective tenderness towards him. The result was that my sadness and isolation lessened a little and I prayed with greater confidence and less resentment for the healing, long-suffering, forgiving love that I so badly needed. And, I believe, it came – through a variety of ways and people.

Love is a living thing which can move and change, flex and tear, which needs exercise and nurture; not a hard-edged, unyielding, unchangeable entity like a stone. And being a living thing, it can be hurt.

**A Silence and a Shouting, Eddie Askew**

Sorrow . . . may sadden your face, but it sharpens your understanding.

**From Ecclesiastes 7**

# BEING THERE

When someone we know is bereaved, we may feel there is little we can do but call in regularly just to be with them. But often the quietly loving presence of another person can relieve some part of the awful isolation, and bring comfort and reassurance.

Being unobtrusively, dependably and caringly present is not, in fact, easy. Among the cards which I treasure from our children are those which say something like: *Thank you for always being there for me.*

Sheila Cassidy, a doctor who was tortured in Chile and now works with those who are terminally ill writes in *The Carer*: 'The dying know we are not God . . . All they ask is that we do not desert them; that we stand our ground at the foot of the cross. At this stage of the journey, of being there, of simply being: it is, in many ways, the hardest.'

Love that is reliable is needed by the walking wounded as well as by the dying. And on a long-term basis. Those who have had their trust abused, for whom 'love' has come to be something hateful, need to experience the reality of love, which is there constantly. Only this long-term reliable and available love can undo damage and heal scars so that love and trust can flower.

Reliability does not imply glamour, and may even seem plain. But far from being dull, endurance and availability are strong and active.

Trust in God at all times, my people.
Tell him all your troubles, for he is our refuge.

**From Psalm 62**

All I can give you I give,
Heart of my heart, were it more,
More would be laid at your feet:
Love that should help you to live,
Song that should spur you to soar.

**A.C. Swinburne**

# PARTNERSHIP

When people are in love, they want to be one with the beloved. They can't take their eyes off each other; at times it's as though they want to eat each other! Physical sexual union is part of this total mutual desire.

I once heard a famous actor speaking about being in love. For him there was nothing to equal it and he would move away from a relationship as soon as its 'first, fine, careless rapture' seemed to be over. And pretty soon he would be trying to recapture the magic with someone else. But this love can only bring in diminishing returns while demanding more and more.

A woman once told me that the quality of intimacy and union that she longed for with her husband was not often achieved within their marriage: their feelings and desires were not fully matched in this respect. But there were many other ways in which he considered and cared for her. And by consciously being aware of and appreciating these, and the rest of his good qualities, she was able to view him and their marriage positively.

This, I believe, can be human love at its best – set within the context of faithfulness and a single-minded commitment to the other person's best interests and true well-being: in other words, loving our neighbour as ourselves. Equally, however, we must not discount the truly wonderful part that physical union can play – especially over many years. This, too, is a loving gift from the Creator, and when it is right, it is as honourable an aspect of loving partnerships as any.

My lover is mine, and I am his.

**From Song of Songs 2**

Our scientific world reduces even love to technique. We see young girls reading massive books on the physiology of sex, and no doubt they could recite a list of erogenous zones, but no one has told them that for the enjoyment of sex, the abandonment of person to person is more important than any artifice.

*The Gift of Feeling*, **Paul Tournier**

Let me not to the marriage of true minds
Admit impediments. Love is not love
Which alters when it alteration finds,
Or bends with the remover to remove:
O, no! it is an ever-fixèd mark,
That looks on tempests and is never shaken.

**Shakespeare**

# THE WHOLE THING

We often hear people blaming politicians for all that's wrong with society, and ministers of religion are told to stick to church affairs and stop meddling in politics. But a religion which is unrelated to all aspects of life has to be about a very small god not worthy of anyone's worship. And, besides, true love cannot be put into compartments. It requires that we function as whole, integrated human beings, no matter what specific 'hat' we may be wearing at any time.

Some years ago, I came across a book marketed for teenagers. As a parent of teenagers myself, I was appalled at the book's contents. And I wondered how those who had published it, and the bookshop manager who had stocked it, could justify having done so. So I wrote as much in a letter to them both.

Their replies gave me the answer. In effect, they had one set of standards and values for their personal, family lives and another for their professional lives.

Living as whole, loving people means *not* separating the two in that way, and so *not* trying to justify putting into the hands of others' children what we would hate anyone to put into the hands of our own.

I know it's not easy to hold together different aspects of our lives – personal and family, professional, social and political. But with true love – God's above all – it can be done. And, for all our sakes, it must be done!

The use of body, mind, emotions and spirit as a totality is the constant challenge for all of us.

**The Capacity to Love, Jack Dominian**

There is one God and Father of all mankind, who is Lord of all, works through all, and is in all.

**From Ephesians 4**

# TRUE FRIENDSHIP

Societies which emphasize the independence of the individual often generate loneliness and isolation. But those in situations where extended families are all-important can have similar feelings too. For real community is not about group size but about whether the individuals involved have good friendships.

Cliquey groups of people who close in together and give the impression of being superior to others have pride and possessiveness to the fore. Whereas genuine friendship is essentially humble, generous and inclusive: a true meeting of mind and spirit, transcending all barriers of class, race, gender or age.

Friends delight in and enjoy each other's company and spiritual — in its widest sense — kinship. They build one another up through praise, affirmation and encouragement; being pleased for each other when things go well and supportive when they don't. And they are outgoing, wanting to turn strangers into friends and bring them in too.

Friendship is a risky business, and also costly, because we can be hurt by opening our hearts to people; and because building and sustaining mutual trust and respect, commitment and understanding, goodwill and good communication, takes much time and effort.

But without friendship our growth is stunted and our lives are — to a great extent — lonely and joyless. Whereas in the context of good friendships and true community there is a deep sense of well-being.

One of the most beautiful qualities of true friendship is to understand and to be understood.

**Seneca**

Friendship can only occur when we give ourself to the other, and to offer ourself to someone else is the most risky of all human endeavours.

*The Friendship Game*, **Andrew M. Greeley**

Two are better off than one, because together they can work more effectively. If one of them falls down, the other can help him up.

**From Ecclesiastes 4**

# CHECKING OUT ATTITUDES

## Anti-love attitudes

self-absorbed, or hating self

hanging on to grudges

afraid to let people get close

afraid of or addicted to change

blinkered by hurt

inward looking, self-absorbed

rigid

hard, scared, defensive

treating others with suspicion

seeing others selfishly

## Love-friendly attitudes

self-accepting, realistic

ready to deal with grudges and forgive

hospitable, wanting closeness

able to face change realistically

able to see clearly

outgoing, identifying with others

stable but flexible

receptive, trusting, vulnerable

treating others with respect

caring about others

| Anti-love attitudes | Love-friendly attitudes |
|---|---|
| apathetic, indifferent | caring, concerned |
| malicious, wanting to harm | well-intentioned, wanting to help |
| idolizing and owning another | wanting to grow together freely |
| 'If you scratch my back, I'll scratch yours.' | giving without strings |
| love if . . . because . . . when . . . | love anyway, regardless; free and unconditional |
| self-protecting | getting involved |
| vain, out for adulation | real and honest with oneself and in relationships |

# FAMILY AFFECTION

Even after our children grew up, we kept up the tradition of making birthday and Christmas lists. One of our son's read: *red/orange shirt, black belt, whistling key-ring*. And then: *woman — one that does what she is told and laughs at my jokes. And agrees with my politics.* Below this our daughter added: *You've got one, it's called your mother.* And below *that*, came my PS: *Dream on!*

This scrap of paper evokes an aspect of affectionate love within our family. Such love takes time to develop — we need to feel safe enough to tease, banter and be playful with one another; to be 'outrageous' even, and know it will be taken well and given a rejoinder in the same vein.

Affection can be conveyed in a whole variety of ways — through words, tone of voice, facial expression and non-sexual hugging, kissing and other forms of touch. In this relaxed, enjoyable atmosphere, we learn about ourselves and one another. We grow more confident and perceptive towards one another.

Also, lest familiarity should breed contempt, we learn to check and balance each other helpfully without being too heavy about it. 'Don't push your luck,' for example, can be said humorously while also dropping the hint that someone is in danger of overstepping the mark, presuming too much or taking advantage.

Families get a very poor press, but I believe the vast majority of them are doing a good job of fostering affectionate love, with the healing, joy and growth that it generates.

You might as well curse your friend as wake him up
early in the morning with a loud greeting.
**From Proverbs 27**

Affection would not be affection if it was loudly and
frequently expressed; to produce it in public is like getting
your household furniture out for a move.
*The Four Loves,* **C.S. Lewis**

# HEALING LOVE

Human beings and our world fall far short of the perfection of love. And healing is vital, particularly for those who have received inconsistent or abusive 'love'.

I'm sure we all know people who are, as the saying goes, their own worst enemy. They complain, for example, that they have no friends, but continue to be thoughtless and abrasive. Or they are constantly exhausted, but keep taking on too much, and burning the candle at both ends.

Some of these need love that is tender but also strong and truthful, before they can – or will – make changes. Through support and friendship, they will be able to behave more constructively. In particular, they will be able to form happier, healthier relationships. And on that basis, real community becomes possible, as does joint, effective action to make our neighbourhood, country and ultimately world, more human and humane, more enjoyable, loving and just.

But healing and change through love take time. For love chooses to work not by force and manipulation but by persuasion, example and consent. Also, change is costly. It takes humility and honesty to admit our need of change and of resources beyond our own. And bringing about that change involves commitment and the willingness to trust and co-operate with others and to receive those resources – in particular, love. This is available from its ultimate source, God, through prayer and, initially or as well, from other people in tune with him.

I may have all the faith needed to move mountains –
but if I have no love, I am nothing.

**From 1 Corinthians 13**

Without the humility and warmth which you have to
develop in your relations to the few with whom you are
personally involved, you will never be able to do anything
for the many.

**Dag Hammerskjöld**

Sustaining, healing and growth are the principal modes of
loving our neighbour, which in turn requires love of self as
its basis.

***The Capacity to Love*, Jack Dominian**

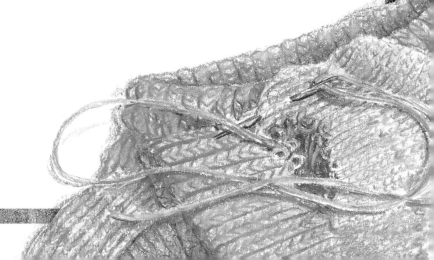

# THE GIFT OF LOVE

When love inspires creativity, the outcome is both moving and enriching, whether we are talking about great artists or simply people who add a special creative touch to whatever they do, particularly in the area of relationships.

I'm thinking of those who excel at creating a relaxed, welcoming space around them; who always remember special dates and send just the right card; who don't care about whose 'turn' it is, but keep initiating or renewing contact, coming up with thoughtful and fun ideas.

Is there love behind the mind-boggling creativity of nature and life? I heard one scientist on the radio likening human history to a massive burp after nature's great meal. Another spoke of the miraculous structure, order and complexity which she saw even in the microscopic details of every cell: indicative, she felt, of some sense of 'love'.

Some look at the broad sweep of nature and life and see only savage competitiveness, with the weakest going to the wall and the fittest and strongest surviving. Others see in it progress through co-operation, with those in isolation losing out and dying off.

In the end our viewpoint reflects the framework by which we live – what 'creed' we have. Within the framework, we should combine what seems reasonable with that which answers our deepest needs and longings. And both mind and heart point me in the direction of a loving Creator and of human creativity as a reflection of that awesome love.

Long ago you created the earth,
and with your own hands you made the heavens.

**From Psalm 102**

Surely it ought not to be true that we, who have the power
with God to obtain by prayer and faith all needed grace,
wisdom and skill, should be bad servants, bad tradesmen,
bad masters.

**George Müller**

# THE PAST

At one point, the recent bushfires in Australia threatened parts of north Sydney and many people suddenly had to leave their homes. They didn't take their cheque books or most expensive possessions with them, however. Instead, they took their photograph albums.

Our past is very precious. Love for the past creates loyalty – to people, ideas and upbringing; it can centre us, direct us and give us confidence in a difficult world.

However, we may also have to *learn* to love parts of our past. I once found myself in tears as I was writing, remembering an incident in my childhood which upset me at the time and which, some thirty years later, was still affecting me painfully! But I knew that blocking out the memory was not the way to reduce its effect on me. Quite the reverse.

As well as sunshine, the past comprises shadows, often very dark ones. Love cannot change the facts of our past, but it can certainly change for the better the way they affect us now. Someone who was bullied at school, for instance, can have his or her self-esteem restored through loving relationships as an adult. Receiving love from friends we value and trust helps us to face painful memories honestly. It puts things in perspective. We can forgive, we can let go.

Love sets us free from the harmful effects of the past. Gradually all of it, good and bad, happy and unhappy, becomes not just something we can live with and revisit without anguish but also a present enrichment, part of our unique identity – and of what we can offer to others.

Forgiveness is not an occasional act; it is a permanent attitude.

**Strength to Love, Martin Luther King**

We know that in all things God works for good with those who love him.

**From Romans 8**

Our aim cannot be to cancel out the past, to try to forget, but to ensure that the strength and meaning which gave beauty to the old patterns is remembered and reinterpreted in the pattern now emerging.

**Cruse Annual Report, Colin Murray Parkes**

# TODAY'S THE DAY

'The gift of the present moment' may be a glib phrase, but there are times when it's easy to see the present as a gift: when we are in love, or have a passion for a particular hobby. Small things can lift our spirits, too – sunshine, a hot bath, a shared joke, a drink with an old friend.

At other times, however, the present feels more like a burden, a pain or a dilemma. We may be doing too much and need to cut down. Our minds as well as our diaries may be over-full. Crowded with turbulent or negative emotions such as fear, anxiety, guilt, anger and envy, we find we're too downcast, preoccupied or drained to be capable of enthusiasm and creativity in the present. And what looks like laziness actually stems from a lack of energy and motivation: we think we are of little account, so what's the point of doing anything?

One way forward is: 'If you can't find love, be loving. If you don't *feel* love, *do* it.' We need to sacrifice, serve, reach out, be kind – both for our own good and for others. Another is be loving to ourselves, allowing those mental and emotional 'tapes' to start playing different messages: we *can* relax, people *aren't* out to get us; some people *like* us, care for us, and would help us. We can make friends with our past and our future, and be set free from their chains – free to live in and value all that the present offers moment by moment.

For me, trusting that God is in loving control of all life is what really gives me freedom in the present. Once we grasp that, we can enjoy all his gifts, now, or in the world to come.

The present moment is all we have; we can only live and love *now*. The only place we can find God is where we are at this moment.

**Heaven in Ordinary**, Angela Ashwin

Yesterday is a cancelled cheque. Tomorrow is a promissory note. Today is ready cash – use it!

**Author unknown**

This is the hour to receive God's favour; today is the day to be saved!

**From 2 Corinthians 6**

# A RICH HARVEST

'When all the people in the world love one another, then the strong will not overpower the weak, the many will not oppress the few, the wealthy will not mock the poor, the honoured will not disdain the humble, and the cunning will not deceive the simple. And it is all due to mutual love that calamities, strifes, complaints, and hatred are prevented from arising.' (Motsi, 4BC)

Throughout history, from every culture, have come visions of a perfect future. Are such visions pipe-dreams? Or are they faint echoes of what could actually be? We can make up our own minds on these questions. But believing in a better future knocks spots off everything else in terms of encouragement and motivation.

Unfortunately, it seems unlikely that utopia will be brought about by human beings within our space or time. No form of government has yet devised, no branch of knowledge has so far discovered, a way to achieve such an ideal fully. Even if we could come up with the perfect system, human beings on their own lack the necessary altruistic, unselfish love that implementing such a system would require.

Our best help, I believe, lies in filling up on God's top-quality, 'unleaded' love, the most user-friendly of all loves and the one that will ultimately prevail. We can then play our part by putting his love to work in our small corner of the world, starting with ourselves and our circle of family, friends, neighbours and acquaintances. Then, step by step, the future may surprise us.

'Supposing a tree fell down, Pooh, when we were underneath it?' asked Piglet.
'Supposing it didn't?' said Pooh, after careful thought.

**The House at Pooh Corner, A.A. Milne**

You give me all I need; my future is in your hands.

**From Psalm 16**

Love is not changed by death,
And nothing is lost and all in the end is harvest.

**From 'Eurydice', Edith Sitwell**

# STRENGTHENED BY LOVE

When I was a child, I thought that being grown up would mean never again feeling small and scared, or having to be told off! I soon realized that a problem-free life, and total physical or emotional security, are impossible in this world. But I also realized that love, above all, helps to cast out fear and to generate the confidence that we need in order to cope with, indeed to enjoy, life.

Such confidence has many aspects. Its agents include people who work with victims of crime, and trauma. A friend told me of a young girl she knew who had been a victim of indecent exposure. The girl was deeply distressed by what had happened, and felt that the world was no longer safe. Men in general merited her anger. As she spoke with a counsellor, she relived the terrible experience. Gradually, over a long period of time, she was able to redraw her map of reality. She regained balance and confidence. Though still wary at times, she recognized that not all men were the same.

There are many ways in which we can help others or allow them to help us – and the confidence created in such situations is always mutual. We need a whole network of relationships which must include people with whom we relate closely and can exchange the more intimate, affectionate forms of care and friendship.

This human love which engenders confidence reaches its full potential when it is resourced by God's love. That is our greatest hope of life and love. And more confident than that, for now, we cannot be.

We are secure. God is running the show. Neither our feelings of depression nor the facts of suffering . . . are evidence that God has abandoned us.

**A Long Obedience in the Same Direction, Eugene Paterson**

There is nothing at all in all creation that will ever be able to separate us from the love of God which is ours through Christ Jesus our Lord.

**From Romans 8**

# Through Different Eyes

Love, we are told, is blind. I disagree. Infatuation may be blind – or at least shortsighted. But real love, I believe, is the lens which corrects distorted vision so that it becomes possible to see clearly, distinguishing background from foreground, main features from incidental detail. In other words, love sees it all and selects what really matters.

A mother I know had a vivid experience of love's transforming clarity. She was glaring at her son's retreating back as he was on the point of slamming out of the house. What she saw was an enraged and difficult adolescent encased in black and aggressively studded at waist, ankle and wrist. But suddenly, her vision cleared and she perceived a needy, confused and hurting human being, caught in the rough weather and ground that lies between childhood and adulthood, and hiding behind an angry armour-plated image.

Seeing people with real love is a way to understand who they really are – to try to stand in their shoes. And when we do that, we see clearly the best way to reach and help them. At the same time, we begin to see the positive potential of apparently negative characteristics: someone capable of deep anger is also capable of deep love, for instance!

It is only with the heart that one can see rightly; what is essential is invisible to the eye.

**_The Little Prince_, Antoine de Saint-Exupery**

The Lord said . . . 'People look at the outward appearance, but I look at the heart.'

**From 1 Samuel 16**

You must see with God's eyes, or I must wear
My furtive failures stark upon my sleeve.

**Basil Dowling**

# WHAT'S IT ALL ABOUT?

A few times in my life, a particular shock or strain has brought on a kind of befogged mental and emotional state – I can't make sense of my thoughts, any book I try to read, or what people are telling me. It's a frightening, nightmarish experience which many, I'm sure, can identify with.

We function best when we're in the opposite frame of mind – one that is purposeful, clear and ordered. Satisfactory relationships and work are what give life meaning for most people on a day-to-day basis. And implicit in both is love: work which we love or people whom we love; ideally, a combination of both.

But so many of us wrestle at times with the larger question of ultimate meaning, and wonder what it's all about. The answers vary from person to person because of differences in temperament, experience and outlook. One can argue the case for life being meaningless, or meaningful – but many are caught between the two viewpoints.

I find it more feasible that our search for meaning reflects the God who made us. He is not a product of mere chance, or a delusion born of our desperation; rather, in our search for meaning he guides and encourages us.

What is the chief end of man? To glorify God and enjoy him for ever.

**From The Shorter Catechism**

We did not invent or create life, our lives, ourselves. If there is a meaning to our lives and our very selves, it must be . . . God-made, not man-made.

*Making Sense out of Suffering*, **Peter Kreeft**

# CHARITY

Sadly, the word charity has become rather negative and is often represented as poor-quality love, cold and dutiful. But it can be love at its best and most complete. Charity is committed and sacrificial compassion and generosity. It has connotations of kindness, selflessness, genuineness, integrity and faithfulness.

It's not love in order to get back approval, admiration or anything else, but a free gift. Not love because of another's lovableness or other attractive qualities, but love from love, self-generating and selfless.

This love is what motivates a parent to hug a vomit-covered child, or to keep reaching out to a disgruntled and rejecting adolescent; the aid worker to dig latrines or risk life and limb to bring food and medical supplies to victims of war; the volunteer to stay and suffer with the dying and the traumatized.

I see charity in the work of the Colombian businessman who rescues children from the sewers of Bogota; of the grandmother who fronts an organization that unilaterally resists terrorism in Northern Ireland; and of the physiotherapist who left her comfortable life and practice to help children suffering from cerebral palsy in Bangladesh.

The supreme example for me is when Jesus was crucified after an unfair trial and, while hanging on the cross, was still able to pray for those who had put him there, 'Forgive them, Father! They don't know what they are doing.'

I am among you as one who serves.
**From Luke 22**

Like your landlord becoming your lodger . . . like
Beethoven queuing up for a ticket to his own concert,
like Picasso painting by numbers, God lived among us.
**Simon Jenkins**

. . . people can only love outside and can only kiss
outside, but Mister God can love you right inside,
and Mister God can kiss you right inside, so he's
different. Mister God ain't like us; we are a little
bit like Mister God, but not much yet.
***Mister God This Is Anna*, Fynn**

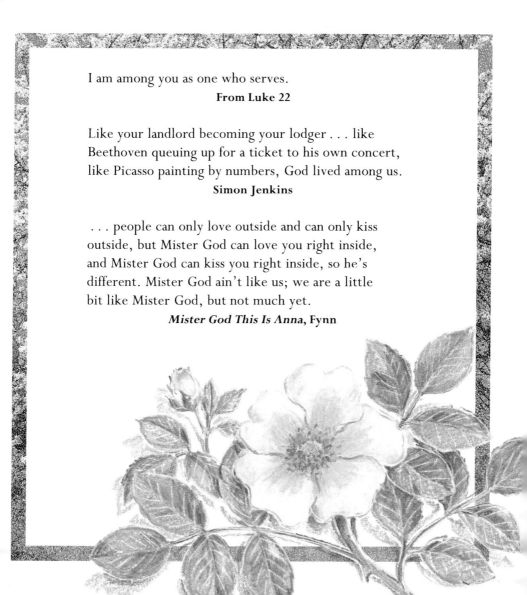

Understanding SECURITY choice friendship

TRUST B·A·L·A·N·C·E JOY warmth

Happiness Accord Blessing

Freedom TRANQUILLITY

MATURITY LOVE SURPRISE!

Zest cheer harmony

peace C·A·L·M life Enthusiasm

HONOUR

BLISS pleasure Delight QUIET

comfort FRESHNESS TENDERNESS

Laughter GROWTH fruition

HEALTH sunshine